itsy bitsy me

My itsy bitsy eyes,
they take a good look.

My itsy bitsy hands,
they almost reach over my head.

My itsy bitsy nose, it smells Mom's fresh bread.

My itsy bitsy fingers
can hold up my bottle.

My itsy bitsy legs
help me walk and waddle.

My itsy bitsy arms,
they can give a big hug.

My itsy bitsy knees
can crawl like a bug.

With my itsy bitsy mouth,
"Thank you" I say.

My itsy bitsy teeth
give the cookie a nibble.

My itsy bitsy toes,
they move and they wiggle.

My itsy bitsy tummy, it fills up with yummies.

On my itsy bitsy back...
"Come for a ride little bunnies!"

My itsy bitsy hair loves a gentle brush.

My itsy bitsy cheeks,
Mom kisses them so much.

My itsy bitsy body, good night!
See you tomorrow!

Do you know who made little itsy bitsy me?

God made my itsy bitsy body.
He made it wonderfully!

More books from iCharacter.org

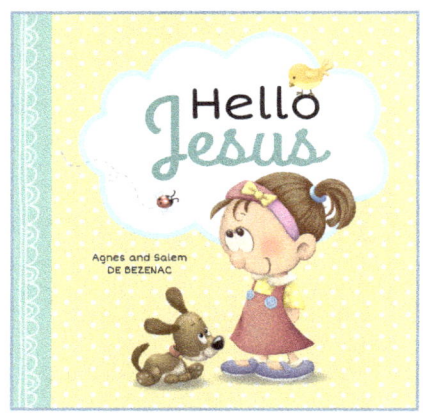

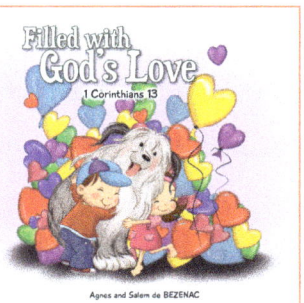

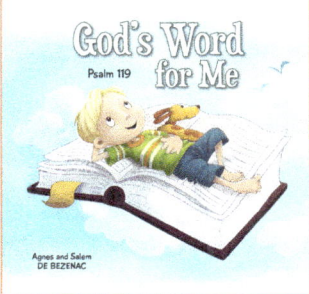

www.iCharacter.org
Published by iCharacter Ltd. (Ireland)
By Agnes and Salem de Bezenac
Illustrated by Agnes de Bezenac
Colored by Henny Y.
Copyright 2019. All rights reserved.

Copyright © 2019 by iCharacter Limited. All rights reserved. No part of this book may be reproduced in any form or by any electronic or mechanical means, including information storage and retrieval systems, without written permission from the publisher or author, except in the case of a reviewer, who may quote brief passages embodied in critical articles or in a review.

www.ingramcontent.com/pod-product-compliance
Lightning Source LLC
Chambersburg PA
CBHW040013080526
44586CB00028B/2992